PIGS IS PIGS

PIGS IS PIGS

ELLIS PARKER BUTLER

WILDSIDE PRESS

PIGS IS PIGS

Originally published in *The American Magazine*, September 1905.

This edition published by Wildside Press LLC.
www.wildsidebooks.com

CONTENTS

PIGS IS PIGS

Mike Flannery, the Westcote agent of the Interurban Express Company, leaned over the counter of the express office and shook his fist. Mr. Morehouse, angry and red, stood on the other side of the counter, trembling with rage. The argument had been long and heated, and at last Mr. Morehouse had talked himself speechless. The cause of the trouble stood on the counter between the two men. It was a soap box across the top of which were nailed a number of strips, forming a rough but serviceable cage. In it two spotted guinea-pigs were greedily eating lettuce leaves.

"Do as you loike, then!" shouted Flannery, "pay for thim an' take thim, or don't pay for thim and leave thim be. Rules is rules, Misther Morehouse, an' Mike Flannery's not goin' to be called down fer breakin' of thim."

"But, you everlastingly stupid idiot!" shouted Mr. Morehouse, madly shaking a flimsy printed book beneath the agent's nose, "can't you read it here — in your own plain printed rates? 'Pets, domestic, Franklin to Westcote, if properly boxed, twenty-five cents each.'" He threw the book on the counter in disgust. "What more do you want? Aren't they pets? Aren't they domestic? Aren't they properly boxed? What?"

He turned and walked back and forth rapidly; frowning ferociously. Suddenly he turned to Flannery, and forcing his voice to an artificial calmness spoke slowly but with intense sarcasm.

"Pets," he said, "P-e-t-s! Twenty-five cents each. There are two of them. One! Two! Two times twenty-five are fifty! Can you understand that? I offer you fifty cents."

Flannery reached for the book. He ran his hand through the pages and stopped at page sixty-four.

"An' I don't take fifty cints," he whispered in mockery. "Here's the rule for ut. 'Whin the agint be in anny doubt regardin' which of two rates applies to a shipmint, he shall charge the larger. The consign-ey may file a claim for the overcharge.' In this case, Misther Morehouse, I be in doubt. Pets thim animals may be, an' domestic they be, but pigs, I'm blame sure they do be, an' me rules says plain as the nose on yer face, 'Pigs, Franklin to Westcote, thirty cints each.' An' Mister Morehouse, by me arithmetical knowledge two times thurty comes to sixty cints."

Mr. Morehouse shook his head savagely.

"Nonsense!" he shouted, "confounded nonsense, I tell you! Why, you poor ignorant foreigner, that rule means common pigs, domestic pigs, not guinea-pigs!"

Flannery was stubborn.

"Pigs is pigs," he declared firmly. "Guinea-pigs, or dago pigs or Irish pigs is all the same to the Interurban Express Company an' to Mike Flannery. Th' nationality of the pig creates no differentiality in the rate, Misther Morehouse! 'Twould be the same was they Dutch pigs or Rooshun pigs. Mike Flannery," he added, "is here to tind to the expriss business an' not to hould conversation wid dago pigs in sivinteen languages fer to discover be they Chinese or Tipperary by birth an' nativity."

Mr. Morehouse hesitated. He bit his lip and then flung out his arms wildly.

"Very well!" he shouted, "you shall hear of this! Your president shall hear of this! It is an outrage! I have offered you fifty cents. You refuse it! Keep the pigs until you are ready to take the fifty cents, but, by George, sir, if one hair of those pigs' heads is harmed I will have the law on you!"

He turned and stalked out, slamming the door. Flannery carefully lifted the soap box from the counter and placed it in a corner. He was not worried. He felt the peace that comes to a faithful servant who has done his duty and done it well.

Mr. Morehouse went home raging. His boy, who had been awaiting the guinea-pigs, knew better than to ask him for them. He was a normal boy and therefore always had a guilty conscience when his father was angry. So the boy slipped quietly around the house. There is nothing so soothing to a guilty conscience as to be out of the path of the avenger.

Mr. Morehouse stormed into the house.

"Where's the ink?" he shouted at his wife as soon as his foot was across the door-sill.

Mrs. Morehouse jumped, guiltily. She never used ink. She had not seen the ink, nor moved the ink, nor thought of the ink, but her husband's tone convicted her of the guilt of having borne and reared a boy, and she knew that whenever her husband wanted anything in a loud voice the boy had been at it.

"I'll find Sammy," she said meekly.

When the ink was found Mr. Morehouse wrote rapidly, and he read the completed letter and smiled a triumphant smile.

"That will settle that crazy Irishman!" he exclaimed. "When they get that letter he will hunt another job, all right!"

A week later Mr. Morehouse received a long official envelope with the card of the Interurban Express Company in the upper left corner. He tore it open eagerly and drew out a sheet of paper. At the top it bore the number A6754. The letter was short. "Subject — Rate on guinea-pigs," it said, "Dr. Sir — We are in receipt of your letter regarding rate on guinea-pigs between Franklin and Westcote, addressed to the president of this company. All claims for overcharge should be addressed to the Claims Department."

Mr. Morehouse wrote to the Claims Department. He wrote six pages of choice sarcasm, vituperation and argument, and sent them to the Claims Department.

A few weeks later he received a reply from the Claims Department. Attached to it was his last letter.

"Dr. Sir," said the reply. "Your letter of the 16th inst., addressed to this Department, subject rate on guinea-pigs from Franklin to Westcote, rec'd. We have taken up the matter with our agent at Westcote, and his reply is attached herewith. He informs us that you refused to receive the consignment or to pay the charges. You have therefore no claim against this company, and your letter regarding the proper rate on the consignment should be addressed to our Tariff Department."

Mr. Morehouse wrote to the Tariff Department. He stated his case clearly, and gave his arguments in full, quoting a page or two from the encyclopedia to prove that guinea-pigs were not common pigs.

With the care that characterizes corporations when they are systematically conducted, Mr. Morehouse's letter was numbered, O. K'd, and started through the regular channels. Duplicate copies of the bill of lading, manifest, Flannery's receipt for the package and several other pertinent papers were pinned to the letter, and they were passed to the head of the Tariff Department.

The head of the Tariff Department put his feet on his desk and yawned. He looked through the papers carelessly.

"Miss Kane," he said to his stenographer, "take this letter. 'Agent, Westcote, N. J. Please advise why consignment referred to in attached papers was refused domestic pet rates.'"

Miss Kane made a series of curves and angles on her note book and waited with pencil poised. The head of the department looked at the papers again.

"Huh! guinea-pigs!" he said. "Probably starved to death by this time! Add this to that letter: 'Give condition of consignment at present.'"

He tossed the papers on to the stenographer's desk, took his feet from his own desk and went out to lunch.

When Mike Flannery received the letter he scratched his head.

"Give prisint condition," he repeated thoughtfully. "Now what do thim clerks be wantin' to know, I wonder! 'Prisint condition,' is ut? Thim pigs, praise St. Patrick, do be in good health, so far as I know, but I niver was no veternairy surgeon to dago pigs. Mebby thim clerks wants me to call in the pig docther an' have their pulses took. Wan thing I do know, howiver, which is they've glorious appytites for pigs of their soize. Ate? They'd ate the brass padlocks off of a barn door! If the paddy pig, by the same token, ate as hearty as these dago pigs do, there'd be a famine in Ireland."

To assure himself that his report would be up to date, Flannery went to the rear of the office and looked into the cage. The pigs had been transferred to a larger box — a dry goods box.

"Wan, — two, — t'ree — four, — foive, — six, — sivin, — eight!" he counted. "Sivin spotted an' wan all black. All well an' hearty an' all eatin' loike ragin' hippy-potty-musses." He went back to his desk and wrote.

"Mr. Morgan, Head of Tariff Department," he wrote. "Why do I say dago pigs is pigs because they is pigs and will be til you say they ain't which is what the rule book says stop your jollying me you know it as well as I do. As to health they are all well and hoping you are the same. P. S. There are eight now the family increased all good eaters. P. S. I paid out so far two dollars for cabbage which they like shall I put in bill for same what?"

Morgan, head of the Tariff Department, when he received this letter, laughed. He read it again and became serious.

"By George!" he said, "Flannery is right. 'Pigs is pigs.' I'll have to get authority on this thing. Meanwhile, Miss Kane, take this letter: "Agent, Westcote, N. J. Regarding shipment guinea-pigs, File No. A6754. Rule 83, General Instruction to Agents, clearly states that agents shall collect from consignee all costs of provender, etc., etc., required for live stock while in transit or storage. You will proceed to collect same from consignee."

Flannery received this letter next morning, and when he read it he grinned.

"Proceed to collect," he said softly. "How thim clerks do loike to be talkin'! Me proceed to collect two dollars and twinty-foive cints off Misther Morehouse! I wonder do thim clerks know Misther Morehouse? I'll git it! Oh, yes! 'Misther

Morehouse, two an' a quarter, plaze.' 'Cert'nly, me dear frind Flannery. Delighted!' Not!"

Flannery drove the express wagon to Mr. Morehouse's door. Mr. Morehouse answered the bell.

"Ah, ha!" he cried as soon as he saw it was Flannery. "So you've come to your senses at last, have you? I thought you would! Bring the box in."

"I hev no box," said Flannery coldly. "I hev a bill agin Misther John C. Morehouse for two dollars and twinty-foive cints for kebbages aten by his dago pigs. Wud you wish to pay ut?"

"Pay — Cabbages — !" gasped Mr. Morehouse. "Do you mean to say that two little guinea-pigs —"

"Eight!" said Flannery. "Papa an' mamma an' the six childer. Eight!"

For answer Mr. Morehouse slammed the door in Flannery's face. Flannery looked at the door reproachfully.

"I take ut the con-sign-y don't want to pay for thim kebbages," he said. "If I know signs of refusal, the con-sign-y refuses to pay for wan dang kebbage leaf an' be hanged to me!"

Mr. Morgan, the head of the Tariff Department, consulted the president of the Interurban Express Company regarding guinea-pigs, as to whether they were pigs or not pigs. The president was inclined to treat the matter lightly.

"What is the rate on pigs and on pets?" he asked.

"Pigs thirty cents, pets twenty-five," said Morgan.

"Then of course guinea-pigs are pigs," said the president.

"Yes," agreed Morgan, "I look at it that way, too. A thing that can come under two rates is naturally due to be classed as the higher. But are guinea-pigs, pigs? Aren't they rabbits?"

"Come to think of it," said the president, "I believe they are more like rabbits. Sort of half-way station between pig and rabbit. I think the question is this — are guinea-pigs of the domestic pig family? I'll ask Professor Gordon. He is authority on such things. Leave the papers with me."

The president put the papers on his desk and wrote a letter to Professor Gordon. Unfortunately the Professor was in South America collecting zoological specimens, and the letter was forwarded to him by his wife. As the Professor was in the highest Andes, where no white man had ever penetrated, the letter was many months in reaching him. The president forgot the guinea-pigs, Morgan forgot them, Mr. Morehouse forgot them, but Flannery did not. One-half of his time he gave to the duties of his agency; the other half was devoted to the guinea-pigs. Long before Professor Gordon received the president's letter Morgan received one from Flannery.

"About them dago pigs," it said, "what shall I do they are great in family life, no race suicide for them, there are thirty-two now shall I sell them do you take this express office for a menagerie, answer quick."

Morgan reached for a telegraph blank and wrote:

"Agent, Westcote. Don't sell pigs."

He then wrote Flannery a letter calling his attention to the fact that the pigs were not the property of the company but were merely being held during a settlement of a dispute regarding rates. He advised Flannery to take the best possible care of them.

Flannery, letter in hand, looked at the pigs and sighed. The dry-goods box cage had become too small. He boarded up twenty feet of the rear of the express office to make a large and airy home for them, and went about his business. He worked with feverish intensity when out on his rounds, for the pigs required attention and took most of his time. Some months later, in desperation, he seized a sheet of paper and wrote "160" across it and mailed it to Morgan. Morgan returned it asking for explanation. Flannery replied:

"There be now one hundred sixty of them dago pigs, for heavens sake let me sell off some, do you want me to go crazy, what."

"Sell no pigs." Morgan wired.

Not long after this the president of the express company received a letter from Professor Gordon. It was a long and scholarly letter, but the point was that the guinea-pig was the Cavia aparoea while the common pig was the genus Sus of the family Suidae. He remarked that they were prolific and multiplied rapidly.

"They are not pigs," said the president, decidedly, to Morgan. "The twenty-five cent rate applies."

Morgan made the proper notation on the papers that had accumulated in File A6754, and turned them over to the Audit Department. The Audit Department took some time to look the matter up, and after the usual delay wrote Flannery that he has had on hand one hundred and sixty guinea-pigs, the property of consignee, he should deliver them and collect charges at the rate of twenty-five cents each.

Flannery spent a day herding his charges through a narrow opening in their cage so that he might count them.

"Audit Dept." he wrote, when he had finished the count, "you are way off there may be was one hundred and sixty dago pigs once, but wake up don't be a back number. I've got even eight hundred, now shall I collect for eight hundred or what, how about sixty-four dollars I paid out for cabbages."

It required a great many letters back and forth before the Audit Department was able to understand why the error had been made of billing one hundred and sixty instead of eight hundred, and still more time for it to get the meaning of the "cabbages."

Flannery was crowded into a few feet at the extreme front of the office. The pigs had all the rest of the room and two boys were employed constantly attending to them. The day after Flannery had counted the guinea-pigs there were eight more added to his drove, and by the time the Audit Department gave him authority to collect for eight hundred Flannery had given up all attempts to attend to the receipt or the delivery of goods. He was hastily building galleries around the express office, tier above tier. He had four thousand and sixty-four guinea-pigs to care for! More were arriving daily.

Immediately following its authorization the Audit Department sent another letter, but Flannery was too busy to open it. They wrote another and then they telegraphed:

"Error in guinea-pig bill. Collect for two guinea-pigs, fifty cents. Deliver all to consignee."

Flannery read the telegram and cheered up. He wrote out a bill as rapidly as his pencil could travel over paper and ran all the way to the Morehouse home. At the gate he stopped suddenly. The house stared at him with vacant eyes. The windows were bare of curtains and he could see into the empty rooms. A sign on the porch said, "To Let." Mr. Morehouse had moved! Flannery ran all the way back to the express office. Sixty-nine guinea-pigs had been born during his absence. He ran out again and made feverish inquiries in the village. Mr. Morehouse had not only moved, but he had left Westcote. Flannery returned to the express office and found that two hundred and six guinea-pigs had entered the world since he left it. He wrote a telegram to the Audit Department.

"Can't collect fifty cents for two dago pigs consignee has left town address unknown what shall I do? Flannery."

The telegram was handed to one of the clerks in the Audit Department, and as he read it he laughed.

"Flannery must be crazy. He ought to know that the thing to do is to return the consignment here," said the clerk. He telegraphed Flannery to send the pigs to the main office of the company at Franklin.

When Flannery received the telegram he set to work. The six boys he had engaged to help him also set to work. They worked with the haste of desperate men, making cages out of soap boxes, cracker boxes, and all kinds of boxes, and as fast as the cages were completed they filled them with guinea-pigs and expressed them to Franklin. Day after day the cages of guinea-pigs flowed in a steady stream from Westcote to Franklin, and still Flannery and his six helpers ripped and nailed and packed — relentlessly and feverishly. At the end of the week they had shipped two hundred and eighty cases of guinea-pigs, and there were in the express office seven hundred and four more pigs than when they began packing them.

"Stop sending pigs. Warehouse full," came a telegram to Flannery. He stopped packing only long enough to wire back, "Can't stop," and kept on sending them. On the next train up from Franklin came one of the company's inspectors. He had instructions to stop the stream of guinea-pigs at all hazards. As his train drew up at Westcote station he saw a cattle car standing on the express company's siding. When he reached the express office he saw the express wagon backed up to the door. Six boys were carrying bushel baskets full of guinea-pigs from the office and dumping them into the wagon. Inside the room Flannery, with his coat and vest off, was shoveling guinea-pigs into bushel baskets with a coal scoop. He was winding up the guinea-pig episode.

He looked up at the inspector with a snort of anger.

"Wan wagonload more an' I'll be quit of thim, an' niver will ye catch Flannery wid no more foreign pigs on his hands. No, sur! They near was the death o' me. Nixt toime I'll know that pigs of whativer nationality is domistic pets — an' go at the lowest rate."

He began shoveling again rapidly, speaking quickly between breaths.

"Rules may be rules, but you can't fool Mike Flannery twice wid the same thrick — whin ut comes to live stock, dang the rules. So long as Flannery runs this expriss office — pigs is pets, — an' cows is pets, — an' horses is pets, — an' lions an' tigers an' Rocky Mountain goats is pets, — an' the rate on thim is twinty-foive cints."

He paused long enough to let one of the boys put an empty basket in the place of the one he had just filled. There were only a few guinea-pigs left. As he noted their limited number his natural habit of looking on the bright side returned.

"Well, annyhow," he said cheerfully, "'tis not so bad as ut might be. What if thim dago pigs had been elephants!"

TEETH IS TEETH

Daniel, the gateman, was sitting on the pine bench before his little square gatehouse, gazing gloomily up the empty stretch of South Fourteenth Street. He was an old man, and having outlived his days of usefulness as an active railroad man had been given the gates at the grade crossing in South Fairview. It was not a lively job. During the middle of the day nothing ever used the track but an occasional bobtail freight, and South Fourteenth Street itself was not lively. Teams avoided the heavy road of loose sawdust, knee-deep over a bed of pine slabs. Morning and evening, to be sure, the sawmill hands passed the gatehouse in a hurrying stream, and some time during the day S. Potts usually dropped over to have a word with Daniel. The days were as long for S. Potts as for Daniel. Except in the morning and evening customers seldom entered his corner saloon, and S. Potts could sit on Daniel's bench and keep an eye on his own door. For five years he had poured upon Daniel the vast stores of his knowedge, and he felt a sort of proprietorship in the old man.

"S. Potts," said Daniel, as his friend look his customary seat on the bench, "I wisht I had turned out to be an inventor, 'stead of a railroad man, I do."

S. Potts settled his long legs comfortably, and shook his head. "Now, there you go, Daniel!" he said reproachfully. "Here I've been teachin' you philosophy for near six years -- just chuckin' it into you free gratis by wholesale, as I might say -- an' still you ain't satisfied."

"I am satisfied, S. Potts," said the old man. "I'm just too satisfied for any use."

"No, you ain't, Daniel," insisted S. Potts. "You're sore an' mad an' discontented, an' it pretty nigh discourages me. Here you are, sixty-four years old, goin' on sixty-five, an' you've got a good job as gateman to this railroad, an' yet you ain't satisfied."

"Yes, I am," insisted Daniel; "yes, I am, S. Potts."

"No, you ain't," S. Potts reasserted, "an' I don't take it as no compliment to me, neither. It ain't everybody that has a chance to associate with me an' hear me talk. You can't claim I've been stingy in giving you free information, Daniel. I've give you enough knowledge to make you equal to Solomon, an' I've learned you philosophy until you ought to be chuck-full of it. But the more I learn you the less you seems to know, an' you keep kickin' all the time."

"You hadn't ought to git mad at me, S. Potts," said Daniel. "You know --"

"I wouldn't blame you so much, Daniel," interrupted S. Potts, "if you didn't have me to talk to, but it does seem, associating with me like you do, an' hearing me talk, you ought to have more sense. Sometimes I think I won't bother with you no more, only I'm so full of knowledge it sort of hurts my head. An' all of it, every drop of it, I pour out on you, Daniel. You ought to be mighty thankful."

"I am thankful," began Daniel, but S. Potts interrupted him again.

"If you was you'd be singing and dancing like a nightingale," he said. "If you knew what was best for you, you would be mighty glad to sit on this bench here an' listen to me talk."

"I am," declared Daniel.

"No, you ain't," insisted S. Potts. "I've knowed you five years, Daniel, and if I had thought it was best for you to be an inventor I'd have made you into one. But I seen you wasn't fitted to be made into an inventor, an' that is why I didn't make you into one. I seen you was fitted to be a gateman, an' I left you be one, didn't I?"

"You did, S. Potts," Daniel admitted.

"I might have made you into an inventor an', sent you off, an' then had somebody with some brains take this job so's I could talk to him an' git some comfort out of it," said S. Potts. "But the minute I seen you I knew that if I made you into an inventor you would go an' invent somethin' to ruin yourself, like Peter Guppy did."

"I'm perfectly satisfied, S. Potts," said Daniel.

"That's the kind of inventor you'd be, the kind Peter Guppy was," continued S. Potts. "He was just sech a discontented old kicker like you are, Daniel, but he was worse off -- he didn't have no S. Potts to be a model to him. He had a nice, steady job sawing wood, an' all he ever had to do was just rest one knee on the sawbuck an' push a saw up an' down all day; no brain work, like the kind that wears me out -- just plain wood-sawing. He had everything to make a man happy, except he didn't have no friend to come across from the saloon an' give him good advice, like you have."

"I'm satisfied," Daniel said, but S. Potts continued:

"No, you ain't, an' he wasn't. He was like you, Daniel. He wanted to invent, an' he looked around to see somethin' to invent that hadn't been invented already, an' what he saw was false teeth. False teeth looked to him like a good thing to invent, because nobody had invented anything very new in false teeth since he could remember."

"Say," exclaimed Daniel enviously, "I wisht I had thought of false teeth! False teeth would be a mighty good thing to invent, wouldn't it, S. Potts?"

"I told you you hadn't no more sense than Peter Guppy had," said S. Potts pitilessly, "but Peter Guppy had more brains than what you have, Daniel. How would you go about inventing false teeth? Just tell me how!"

Daniel gazed at the sawdusty level of South Fourteenth Street, and creased his tanned forehead into thoughtful wrinkles. He shifted uneasily on his bench, and frowned hard. "Well, of course, I can't say right off like this," he said at length, "but if I had time --"

"The reason nobody had been gittin' up new inventions in false teeth," interrupted S. Potts, "was the same then as it is today -- false teeth was already as good as they could be made. But Peter Guppy was like you, always complainin' an' unsatisfied, so he went an' had the few old teeth he had left in his head pulled out, an' had a good set of false ones made -- double set, uppers an' lowers -- an' he used to set on his saw-buck day after day with them false teeth in his hand, studyin' 'em an' studyin' 'em, an' wonderin' how he could improve on 'em. An' at night he would sigh, an' go to bed, an' then he couldn't sleep for thinkin' of them false teeth. He was about three years thinkin' how to invent better false teeth."

"It was worth it, it was worth it!" said Daniel enthusiastically.

"Three years," said S. Potts, "that was the time that Peter Guppy put in settin' around holdin' his uppers an' lowers in his hand. Sometimes he would hold the uppers in one hand an' the lowers in the other, an' sometimes he would hold them all in one hand an' scratch his head with the other, an' all the while he was gittin' more an' more discouraged. They ain't nothin' more disheartenin' than to set day after day studyin' false teeth. The more you look at 'em the more they look just like what they always looked like. But Peter Guppy was just sech a fool as you are, Daniel. He hadn't no sense."

"Well, S. Potts, we can't all be --" began Daniel.

"He was lazy, that's what he was," said S. Potts. "He wanted to git rich quick, like you do. He'd set by the day with them uppers an' lowers in his hand, openin' an' shuttin' his hand so them teeth would champ open an' shut before his eyes, an' when he got tired in his right hand he would shift them teeth over into his left hand an' go on champin' 'em. So one day he says: 'I declare to goodness, if it's goin' to take ma forty years to invent somethin' new about these here teeth, I wisht there was some way the plaguy things could do their own champin'! My hands is 'most wore out champin' the plaguy things.' An' right there, Daniel, was where he got the idee."

"I can almost see it, S. Potts," said Daniel.

"Power!" said S. Potts. "Power! That's what he thought of. That's what a lazy man always thinks of first off -- gittin' power to do his work for him. First off Peter Guppy thought he'd hire a boy to champ his teeth for him, whilst all he had to do would be to lay back an' look on; but he didn't have no money to hire a boy. Then he thought what a fine thing it would be to have self-workin' teeth that would champ by machinery whilst he looked on, an' then he stood up an' yelled. He'd thought what he could invent about false teeth. He could invent self-operatin' teeth. Nobody had ever invented self-operatin' teeth, so far as he knew."

"I wisht I had thought of that invention," said Daniel greedily.

"I bet you do," said S. Potts. "That's about what sense you've got. But it wasn't much to invent. I could have thought of it long before Peter Guppy did, but I seen it was a foolish thing to invent, so I didn't think of it. Anybody could have seen that the only way to improve a perfect thing like false teeth was to put power into them, but I wouldn't do it. No, sir! But Peter Guppy went right ahead an' done it. He set right to work an' invented Guppy's Auxiliary Motor Teeth, an' was as proud as pie. Soon as I seen 'em I shook my head. I hated to discourage him, but I hadn't no faith in self-actin' teeth, so I just hiked up my head an' shook it. But it didn't do no good.

"I guess he made a lot o' money, didn't he?" asked Daniel wistfully.

"Out of an invention I had shook my head at?" questioned S. Potts scornfully. "Peter Guppy thought he would make a lot of money. That's what he thought. Them teeth looked all right, an' they would have fooled you, Daniel. They was rigged up with a clockwork spring, an' when Peter Guppy touched a button they went right to work an' chewed. Just like I'm openin' an' shuttin' my hand here -- champ, champ, champ! That's the way they worked when Peter Guppy held 'em in his hand. He was all swelled up about 'em. He figgered they'd save a lot of labor, an' lots of time, too, because all a feller had to do was push his food into his mouth, an' them teeth would do the chewin'. Peter Guppy was mighty proud."

"I'd be proud," said Daniel.

"I wasn't," said S. Potts. "I waited. Peter Guppy went around town tellin' how he was the greatest benefactor America ever had, an' that all this nation had needed was him to invent them teeth, an' now it would be the happiest on earth, he said everybody knew that what was the matter with America was indigestion an' dyspepsia, caused by lack of not chewin' their food enough, caused by lack of time for eatin'. Now, he said, folks wouldn't have to chew long, they could chew quick. They could set their teeth at high speed, an' the teeth would chew sixty bites a second, or if they wanted to git some satisfaction chewin' tobacco or gum they could set the teeth at low speed an' chew long an' steady. All lazy people would have to do would be to set with their mouths open an' let the Guppy Auxiliary Motor Teeth go ahead an' chew. Peter Guppy used to stand down at the post-office corner an' place them teeth on the sidewalk an' set 'em goin', an' the whole crowd would stand off an' admire 'em whilst they champed away, sixty bites to the second, as regular as clockwork."

"What'd he put 'em on the sidewalk for, S. Potts?" asked Daniel.

"They was safest there," said S. Potts. "Peter Guppy had let 'em champ so much in his hand that the muscles of his hand was all tired out, an' he was afraid they might champ out of his hand an' fall an' git broken; but on the sidewalk they just champed around in a circle, goin' kind o' hippety-hop. They traveled backward like a crab, but the action was more like a clamshell, only quicker. You don't often see a clamshell open an' shut sixty opens an' sixty shuts to the second, Daniel."

"I don't recall none," said Daniel. "Why didn't he use them teeth in the regular way."

"There was one bad thing about them teeth," said S. Potts. "They had to have room in 'em for the spring, an' that made 'em step mos' too high when he had 'em in his mouth. Peter had only about a two-inch-high mouth, an' them teeth was three-inch steppers. They sort o' strained his mouth. There ain't nothin' much worse in false teeth than to have 'em tread too high, 'specially when they tread by machinery. It used to tire Peter all out, openin' an' shuttin' his mouth that way, sixty times to the second, an' them teeth used to knock so hard on the roof of his mouth that he had to sit at meals with one hand on the top of his head to hold hisself down, an' even then he bounced so hard on the chair that he jarred the house some. The whole neighborhood could tell when Peter was havin' a little nourishment. He made a noise like a motorboat. Them that seen him said it was sort o' funny to see him, settin' back with his mouth wide open an' them teeth jiggin' away inside of it. Often he used to joggle clean off onto the floor, an' if he didn't grab the table-leg with his free hand he would joggle all 'round the room. I wouldn't have had the things at no price."

"Neither would I," said Daniel.

"Yes, you would," said S. Potts. "You would if I hadn't been there to stop you. You would have gone an' bought a pair, like as not. 'Twould have been just like you to sleep with the blame things in your mouth, like Peter did. That's what spoiled Peter's looks. He'd been a fair looker before that, but one night he went to bed with them teeth in his mouth, an' they got touched off accidental whilst he was asleep, an' they champed all night, an' the next morning Peter had the top of his mouth all blistered, except where them teeth had worn calluses, an' his lower jaw was pushed down so far out of plumb that it was permanently lowered, an' all the rest of his life he had to go 'round lookin' like a big-mouth bass out of water. He couldn't git his mouth shut by an inch. No, sir! You bet he never wore them teeth to bed again!"

"Took 'em out nights, I reckon," said Daniel.

"He took 'em out," said S. Potts, "but he didn't do like he ought to have done an' put 'em outside the house. He laid 'em on the stand by his bed, an' woke up dreamin' they was stole, an' when he put out his hand to see if they was there they bit him on the finger. They bit him three times before he could git his finger out, an' he was so mad he grabbed 'em an' threw 'em across the room, an' they lit on the sofa an' chewed a sofa-pillow till daybreak. When Peter got up in the morning there wasn't nothin' left of the sofa-pillow but fine feather dust, an' the teeth had chewed on through the sofa, an' fell to the floor an' chewed the hind leg of the sofa clean off. Peter's wife was so mad she never smiled again until she got his insurance money. Peter died from them teeth."

"I s'pose," said Daniel thoughtfully, "I s'pose that when them teeth bit Peter they give him the hydrophoby."

S. Potts looked at him sorrowfully. "Ef that ain't just like you, Daniel!" he said. "There ain't no logic in you. Of course if this was a pack an' parcel o' lies I was tellin' you, it might be that I'd go on an' say Peter Guppy got the hydrophoby from that bite, but nothin' of that kind happened. Natchurally. Because them was Peter's own teeth what bit him. If Peter had had hydrophoby when them teeth bit him then they would have give it to him, like as not, but he didn't have. The trouble was that he swallered them teeth. I don't suppose you know anything about physiology, Daniel?"

"Well," S. Potts," said Daniel apologetically, "I ain't looked into it much. You ain't never told me much about -- what did you say that word was, S. Potts?"

"Physiology," said S. Potts. "But if you don't know nothin' about it, it ain't much use tellin' you about what happened to Peter Guppy, "cause you wouldn't understand it. I don't reckon you know what an esophagus is, even?"

"Now, S. Potts," began Daniel pleadingly, "you know I never had any esoph--"

"Daniel," said S. Potts, "an esophagus is a sort of knob on the inside of your throat, that's what it is. It's put there to help you swaller. But the whole inside of Peter Guppy's throat was spread wide by the constant champin' of them teeth, an' where the back end of them rubbed, his esophagus was worn down to a nubbin. So that's how it happened that whilst Peter Guppy was goin' downtown one day he swallered his teeth. He threw his head back to sneeze, an' whilst his mouth was open them teeth slipped on down his throat. That wouldn't have been much loss. Them teeth was a failure, an', anyway, if Peter Guppy had wanted to have a pair he could have rigged up another, but on the way down the push-button bumped against his esophagus, an' it set them teeth goin'. Never shall I forgit that scene, Daniel, an' I hope it will be a lesson to you."

"I hope so, S. Potts," said Daniel.

"I hope so, but I doubt it," said S. Potts. "I heard poor Peter yell, an' I run, an' so did everybody, an' there was poor Peter layin' on the ground, writhin' in agony, an' nobody knowed what was the matter. Some thought he was havin' a fit, and some thought maybe he was inventin' some new invention. Then all of a sudden we seen a little lump rise by his left knee, an' out come them teeth. Whilst we was all dumfounded, they sort of looked around an' give a champ or two, an' jumped right at Peter's other leg, an' disappeared, sixty champs to the second. There wasn't much we could do. Some said one thing an' some said another, but any of them wouldn't have done no good; if so I would have done it. You know that, Daniel. When the sun went down there wasn't nothin' left of Peter Guppy but one shoe, an' them Auxiliary Motor Teeth had begun on that, sixty bites to a second. But I stopped that right then."

"I bet you did, S. Potts," said Daniel enthusiastically. "I bet you did."

"I did," said S. Potts. "'Here,' I says, teeth has had fun enough, an' it's time they stopped. We'd best stop 'em whilst there's enough of Peter Guppy left to have a funeral with.' That's what I said, but I had to git an ax before I could kill them teeth, an' then they nearly sprang on me an' bit me. But I was just a little too quick for 'em."

"There ain't no false teeth goin' to git the best of you, S. Potts," said Daniel admiringly. "But it does seem sort of too bad that they had to be killed off. They might have --"

"There you go!" said S. Potts. "If that ain't just like you! Why, them teeth was murderers! That's what they was -- murderers!"

Daniel shook his head regretfully. "I'd liked to have seen 'em, S. Potts," he said. "If you hadn't killed 'em that way maybe I might have seen 'em, an' if I had seen 'em I might have knowed how to invent 'em a little better. Of course they was murderers, but you might have sort of arrested 'em -- put 'em in the penitentiary. Them teeth oughtn't to have been killed that way with an ax, S. Potts, even if you did do it. They ought to have been arrested an' tried. They ought to have had a fair trial,"

"Well, it ain't much use tellin' you things, Daniel," said S. Potts with disgust. "Seems to me like Peter Guppy give them teeth all the trial they deserved. I bet you don't even see the moral what this talk has got in it for you. Do you, now?"

Old Daniel wrinkled his brow and thought deeply. Suddenly he smiled. "Sure I do!" he said. "Sure I do, S. Potts! When a feller invents Auxiliary Motor Teeth he don't want to use 'em; he wants to sell 'em to other folks."

"Great howling Christmas candles!" said S. Potts, and he got up and went back to his saloon.

Made in the USA
Las Vegas, NV
08 March 2024

86884759R00018